CW00531410

Gautama Buddha

An imprint of Om Books International

First published in 2017 by

An imprint of Om Books International

Corporate & Editorial Office
A 12, Sector 64, Noida 201 301
Uttar Pradesh, India
Phone: +91 120 477 4100
Email: editorial@ombooks.com
Website: www.ombooksinternational.com

Sales Office
107, Ansari Road, Darya Ganj,
New Delhi 110 002, India
Phone: +91 11 4000 9000
Fax: +91 11 2327 8091
Email: sales@ombooks.com
Website: www.ombooks.com

ISBN : 978-93-84225-07-0

Printed in India

10 9 8 7 6 5 4 3 2 1

Contents

Birth and Early Life

This is the story of Gautama Buddha, one of the greatest religious thinkers and teachers of all times. The details of his life are based on stories and tradition because the first written accounts date from about 200 years after his death.

An interesting fact is that he was not called Buddha when he was born. At that time he was called Siddhartha Gautam and to know all about his life, one has to start at the point when he was born.

More than 2,500 years ago, Siddhartha Gautam was born to King Suddhodhana, the head of the Shakya tribe, and Queen Maya. There are several stories related to his birth. According to one of them, one full moon night Queen Maya had a strange dream. She dreamt that four angels carried her to a lake in the Himalayas. After bathing her in the lake, they

clothed her in heavenly clothes, anointed her
with perfumes and bedecked her with flowers.
A big, white elephant, carrying a white
lotus in its trunk, came to Maya and walked
around her three times and entered her womb
through the right side. Then it struck her on
the right side with its trunk and vanished into
thin air!

The queen was surprised. She told the king about her dream. He called 64 priests to his court and asked them to explain it. The Brahmins discussed among themselves and

informed the royal couple that a son would be born to them but he would leave home at an early age. They also said that if this did not happen, he would become a world conqueror. But if he left home, he would become "the Buddha".

It is believed that Queen Maya left Kapilavatthu, the capital, to go to her childhood home, Devadaha, to give birth to her child. A royal palanquin, carried by a thousand courtiers, was brought to carry her there.

A palanquin was a covered box with comfortable seats inside and draped in curtains. It had four long wooden 'arms' that were used by four men who carried the palanquin on

their shoulders. This was the common mode of travel, especially by the women of royal homes. It is important to remember that in those days there were no cars, buses or trains so this was the way people traveled, even long distances.

14

While they were on their way, the royal procession passed Lumbini Grove, which was full of blossoming trees. Queen Maya was fascinated by the sight of the lovely flowers and asked her courtiers to stop. She left the palanquin and entered the grove. It was in this beautiful garden at Lumbini that prince Siddhartha was born.

The queen and the baby were showered with perfumed blossoms, and two streams of sparkling water poured from the sky to bathe them.

And, as legends go, the infant stood
up, and took seven steps, and proclaimed
"I alone am the World-Honoured One!"

19

Queen Maya returned to Kapilavatthu, but sadly enough, she died soon after the birth of her son. This was, indeed, very unfortunate and the infant prince was nursed and raised by the queen's sister Prajapati, who was also married to King Suddhodhana.

The Four Sights

King Suddhodhana could not forget what the holy men had prophesied: that the prince would either become a great military conqueror or a great spiritual teacher. Now, the king wished that his son should be a great warrior, so he began

training him accordingly. He wanted to make sure that there was no outside influence on the child and he stayed sheltered from the outside world.

He raised the boy in great luxury and shielded him completely from knowledge of religion and human suffering. Prince Siddhartha led a protected life and became 29 years old with little experience of the world outside the walls of his palaces.

One day, wanting to see the outside world, Prince Siddhartha asked a charioteer to take him on a ride through the countryside. Soon, he made this a habit and would go off on rides into the town. On one of these trips, he was shocked by the sight of an aged man, then a sick man, and then a dead body. Till then, he had led a sheltered life, without any knowledge of the tragedies of life. Now, the stark realities

of old age, disease, and death saddened him deeply. He felt very sad to learn that life was not just a bed of roses; there were many thorns in it too! Siddhartha recognized that no matter how rich or important a person might be, all beings were finally subject to disease and death. These final realities, suffering and death could not be wished away.

Finally, one day, he saw a wandering ascetic or 'sadhu' or Samana as they were called. Prince Siddhartha couldn't understand who the man was or why he looked the way he did. He asked the charioteer who explained that the ascetic was a person who had left home and gone out to seek the truth of life. This was also called giving up or 'renouncing' the world, in order to find

peace and also the answers to many questions on life and death. The final aim of such people, said the charioteer to the young prince, was to find release from the chain of death and suffering. These sadhus had left their home forever, and had taken up the begging bowl and staff, to seek an end from the cycle of birth and rebirth. Siddhartha was deeply moved by all this information and kept thinking about them all the time.

These sights that he saw over a period of time came to be called the "Four Sights."

The Renunciation

The Prince returned to palace life, but his heart was not in it. He did not enjoy the luxuries that were available to him. At this time, his wife, Yashodhara, gave birth to a son but even this happy event did not make him glad. The child was called Rahula which means "fetter" or chain but could not tie down the wanderer in his father. With every passing day, Siddhartha became more and more restless.

Visions of the old, the sick and the dead haunted him; the option of becoming a 'samana', and finding the answers to the sufferings of man, became a strong feeling within. His wife, Yashodhara, sensing how disturbed he was, tried her best to draw his attention to his little son but Siddhartha was not to be distracted from the path he had chosen for himself.

One night, he walked alone through the palace. The comforts that he had once loved seemed awful! He could see that many musicians and dancing girls, tired after performing, had fallen asleep and were sprawled all over the place. They were snoring and presented an ugly sight. Looking at these people, Prince Siddhartha reflected on the truths he had discovered and felt that one day, old age, disease, and death would overtake all of them and turn their bodies to dust. Once again, he was overcome with a strong desire to leave it all, go out into the world, and find answers to these problems of life.

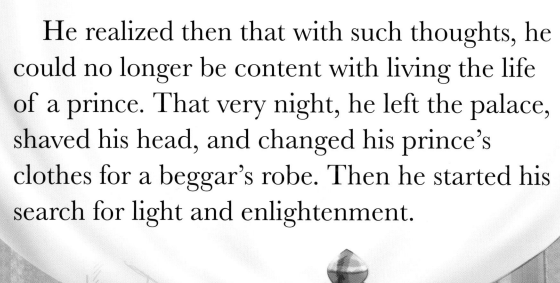

He realized then that with such thoughts, he could no longer be content with living the life of a prince. That very night, he left the palace, shaved his head, and changed his prince's clothes for a beggar's robe. Then he started his search for light and enlightenment.

For six years, Siddhartha roamed around like a sadhu, traveling through the cities of the Gangetic plain. He studied the lives of teachers who would help him in learning disciplines that would end his 'samsara'. He learned yogic meditation and other practices but felt that they gave only partial relief that did not last long.

He believed that man was capable of achieving much higher goals. He stopped eating food, in order to teach himself self-discipline and became very thin, but concluded that this only added to his misery, it did not release one from it.

Searching for Truth

Siddhartha knew that the best place to start finding the answers that were still not within reach was at the feet of learned men and teachers. So he began by searching for famous teachers, who taught him about the

many religions of his day. They explained the philosophies that were current at the time, and taught him how to meditate. But even after spending time with them and listening to them, Siddhartha felt that there were many doubts and questions that still remained in his mind. So he and five of his followers, or 'disciples' as they were called, left to find enlightenment by themselves.

During this time, all six of them tried to find release from suffering through strict physical discipline. They would bear all kinds of pain: holding their breath, fasting nearly to starvation simply in order to exercise control. But Siddhartha was still not satisfied. There

was an emptiness that was still not filled. From one extreme of luxuries, he had moved to the complete opposite: he had embraced pain and 'self-mortification' or suffering. This was definitely not what he had started looking for. What he had wanted was the best option, the Middle Way between those two extremes.

He remembered an experience from his childhood, when his mind had settled into a state of deep peace. He realized that instead of starvation, he needed nourishment to build up his strength for the effort. Siddhartha remembered an incident from his early life when he had felt at peace with himself. And suddenly he realized that the path of liberation was through discipline of mind. To discipline the mind, one did not need to starve the body and there was no wisdom in doing this. But when he accepted a bowl of rice milk from a young girl, his companions assumed he had given up the quest for truth and left him.

Enlightenment

According to the Buddhist tradition, Siddhartha sat beneath a huge tree that was later called the "Wisdom," or "Bodhi" tree and vowed not to leave it until he achieved the knowledge he was seeking. He sat down and started thinking deeply or 'meditating.'

Siddhartha thought deeply about 'mindfulness' —awareness—of mind and body. As a child, he used to often meditate and focus on his breath and that had brought him a sense of calmness. At the same time, it had also given him a sense of awareness. Remembering this, he undertook a long period of meditation that ended in his learning a great deal about human nature and human condition. Finally, he attained nibbana (or nirvana) – the understanding that liberated him from 'samsara.'

It was then that he earned the title of the 'Buddha – the Awakened or the Enlightened One.'

It is believed that for 49 days, he enjoyed this liberation, before deciding to teach others how to follow his example of attaining 'nirvana.'

Teachings and Sermons

To start with, the Buddha did not want to teach, as he felt that what he had experienced could not possibly be explained in or conveyed through words. This could be done only through strict discipline, which was difficult to follow. Simply listening without any experience would not be useful and his teachings would be misunderstood. All these thoughts prevented the Buddha from teaching right away. It was only later that his kindness and keenness to share with the world what he had discovered, persuaded him to make the attempt.

The first place he went to was the Deer Park in what is now called Sarnath near Varanasi in Uttar Pradesh. There he found the five companions who had left him. They could immediately see that something had changed in him, and, following his Dhamma (Dharma: teachings) became the first arahants of Buddhism. He preached his first teaching or 'sermon' before them. This sermon centers on the Four Noble Truths. Stated very simply, these truths were:

1. Life is full of sorrows; suffering continues through an endless chain of rebirths.

2. Sorrows are caused because of our greed or wants.

3. If we overcome our greed, we will not be sad.

4. For doing this, we should follow the Eightfold Path preached by the Buddha.

The Buddha devoted himself to teaching wherever he went. He attracted hundreds of followers. Wherever he went, people flocked to see him and hear him speak. His speeches, or 'sermons' as they were called, became very popular. Buddha taught for many years and his followers grew each day.

Last Words

Towards the end of his life, Lord Buddha
made up with his father, King Suddhodhana.
He also met his devoted wife, Yashodhara, who
had become a nun and a disciple. Rahula, his
son, became a novice monk at the young age of
7 and spent the rest of his life with his father.

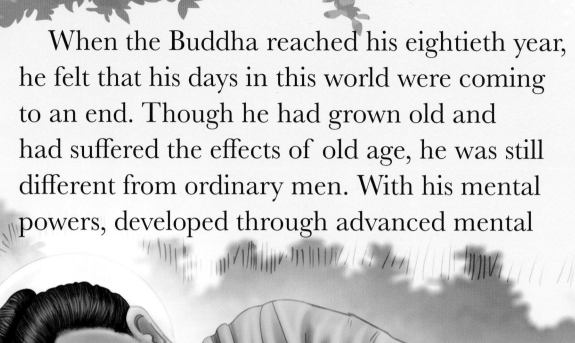

When the Buddha reached his eightieth year, he felt that his days in this world were coming to an end. Though he had grown old and had suffered the effects of old age, he was still different from ordinary men. With his mental powers, developed through advanced mental

training, he was able to overcome
pain. His mind was always alert and
his thoughts clear, even though his
body was beginning to weaken.

This means that every creation will die one day. It is up to each person to work out a way of freedom from sorrow by hard work and discipline.

Birth of Buddhism

In the last year of his life, he decided to spend his days in the peaceful and simple surroundings of Kusinaga, a small village in northern India. At the age of 80, Lord Buddha became very ill. His last words, as is generally believed, were:

"All compounded things are subject to decay, work out your salvation with diligence."

The Four Noble Truths led to the birth of the Eightfold Path preached by Gautama Buddha. These eight guiding principles, if followed, would release human beings from all sorrows and give them freedom from the endless cycle of birth and rebirth. In other words, they would get 'Nirvana'.

The Eightfold Path that Lord Buddha asked everyone to follow taught correct behaviour and discipline. It said that everyone should practise:

Right view

Right intention

Right speech

Right action

Right livelihood

Right effort

Right mindfulness

Right concentration

What he preached was that if one led a
life where all of the above were followed in
the correct manner, one would gain freedom
from the cycle of births and deaths and attain
nirvana.

Buddhism was more a way of life than a
religion. Though it was seen as one at the time,
all it did was teach human beings to stick to
correct beliefs, views and actions and lead a
simple life. It discouraged rituals and believed in
simple faith and action. One reason it became
popular was because it went against the caste-
system, which was a part of Hinduism. Society

66

was divided into classes on the basis of caste and the lower caste people had no rights and led a very hard life. Buddhism came as a breath of fresh air to such people, as it gave them the freedom to live a life that gave them equal status. This was a release from hundreds of years of being considered 'outcastes' and being looked down upon.

Spread of Buddhism

During Lord Buddha's life, Sanghas or committees were formed to enable the spread of Buddhism. These committees held regular meetings and educated people on the Middle Path. Many kings of the time converted to Buddhism and this led to its spread in other parts of Asia. The Mauryan king, Aśoka, did a lot for the growth of this religion. He supported

Buddhist teachings and became the ideal Buddhist king. Some historical accounts report that during Aśoka's reign, the Third Buddhist Council was held at Pātaliputra in 250 BCE. Soon afterward, Buddhist missionaries travelled to countries outside India, possibly as a result of the policies set at Pātaliputra.

Aśoka's son Mahindra went to Sri Lanka as a Buddhist missionary. A form of Buddhism called 'Theravāda Buddhism' later spread from Sri Lanka to the Southeast Asian lands of Burma (Myanmar), Siam (Thailand), Laos, and Cambodia. Buddhism is believed to have entered China in the 3rd century, and 'Mahāyāna Buddhism' became one of the main religions in China, Japan, Korea, and Vietnam.

Buddhist statues and paintings became central to the arts in these lands. Monasteries became a basic part of social institutions throughout Asia. Political ideas, such as views on the nature of kingship, were often based on concepts of the Buddhist ruler.

Decline of Buddhism

By the end of the seventh century, the very things that had made Buddhism attractive to people began changing. A kind of class-system crept into it, rituals and sacrifices were practised and even idol worship, something that the lord had preached strongly against, became a part of it. In fact, Lord Buddha's statues began to

be worshipped openly! All these changes had a negative impact on the popularity of the religion. Apart from this, a lot of internal differences crept in among the Sanghas and these factors led to the gradual decline of this religion, which had taught people a new way of life.

However, despite the decline in numbers, Buddhism is still alive in many parts of the world, particularly in countries like Thailand, Sri Lanka, Myanmar, Cambodia, Laos, Japan, China and in some parts of India and Nepal. Everywhere, the fast pace and high stress of modern life has led to people becoming

interested in the peaceful philosophy of Buddhism. In particular, there is a very deep interest in learning how to meditate, both to overcome stress and anxiety, and to deepen one's spiritual experience.

As long as the desire to lead a simple, disciplined life remains in the human heart, the teachings of Lord Buddha will stay alive in some form or the other.

OTHER TITLES IN THIS SERIES

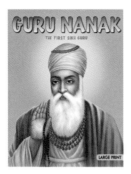

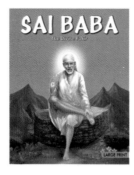

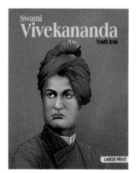

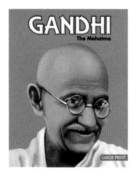

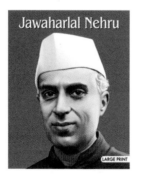

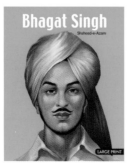

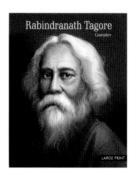